MW00777363

IDLER BOOKS

Idle Thoughts

Tom Hodgkinson is editor of the *Idler* magazine and author of several books including *How to Be Idle*, *How to Be Free*, *The Idle Parent* and *Business for Bohemians*. He lives in London. Sign up for his free newsletter at idler.co.uk.

How to Be Idle
How to Be Free
The Idle Parent
The Book of Idle Pleasures (*with Dan Kieran*)
The Ukulele Handbook (*with Gavin Pretor-Pinney*)
Business for Bohemians
How to Live in the Country
An Idler's Manual

IDLE
THOUGHTS

Letters on Good Living

Tom Hodgkinson

Illustrated by Alice Smith
Idler snail by Ged Wells

IDLER BOOKS
MMXXIV

First published in 2024
by Idler Books

Great Western Studios,
65 Alfred Road
London W2 5EU

ISBN 978-1-7390944-1-6

FIRST EDITION

Illustrations by Alice Smith

Typesetting by Bracketpress

Print managed by Adam Shaw Associates

For Arthur

Contents

Introduction

Dear Idlers,

The following forty short squibs were first released as newsletters. Each week, I send a "Letter from the Editor" to a worldwide audience of layabouts and freedom seekers.

Together we attempt to wrestle, gently, with that great philosophical question: how to live. My reflections are sometimes prompted by things in the news, and sometimes by a trivial event in my own life – an argument or something I've read in a book – and sometimes by a comment from a reader.

We've put them together in this little book, just right for handbag or pocket.

I hope you enjoy it.

Tom Hodgkinson
London, February 2024

1

On Diogenes and Antiwork

THE AMERICAN "antiwork" movement – or at least its most visible expression, a forum on Reddit – has grown to the point at which even the *Today* programme and the *Financial Times* have taken notice. I'm a lover of the *FT*, even though I don't understand it or feel much fondness for the greedy old white guys you've never heard of who dominate its pages. Today I read the following baffling but strangely beautiful headlines: "Short sellers tuck into Beyond Meat"; "Mishcon de Reya: City law firm's IPO roadshow gets off to a bumpy start"; "TPG's IPO cements fee shift for private equity firms going public"; "Rocco Commisso bought a football club. Then the trouble started"; "Flipdish valued at $1bn in Tencent-led funding round". (Isn't Tencent a rapper? Certainly sounds like one.)

Anyway, Reddit's "antiwork" forum clearly has a lot in common with the *Idler*. The people who post things on it call themselves "idlers" for one thing, and they like the same people. One of their heroes is the US academic Benjamin Hunnicutt, who wrote a great book called *Free Time* which documents the two-centuries-old campaign to reduce working hours. "We maybe consider that there might be an alternative to living our lives in thrall to the wealthiest among us, serving their profit," he said. "Maybe there are other things to do with our lives than piling up profits for those that are ultra-rich, and taking that time, reclaiming that time." In other words, stop working for the kind of people you read about in the *FT* and do something you want to do instead.

The original "antiwork" philosophers were people like Socrates and Diogenes, who wandered around ancient Athens doing very little. One story goes that Diogenes, who was nicknamed the "dog-philosopher", had only one possession, a wooden bowl. He was going for a walk in the woods and came across a peasant boy who was kneeling by a stream and drinking water from it, using his cupped hands. On seeing this admirable example of self-sufficiency, Diogenes looked at his bowl, said, "What an absurd encumbrance!" and flung it into the distance.

Socrates was not quite as extreme but appeared to live reasonably well despite not having a job. He certainly had a lot of fun drinking wine and talking with his mates Alcibiades and Aristophanes, though his wife Xanthippe reputedly emptied a chamber pot over his head when he rolled up one morning after an all-nighter. The antiwork or philosophical life doesn't always, perhaps, sit happily with the demands of family.

When you start looking, "antiwork" thinkers are everywhere. Nineteenth-century anarchists and socialists such as the generously bearded Kropotkin and William Morris used the term "wage slavery" to describe miserable jobs that people did simply for the money. This was also of course the century of Blake's "dark satanic mills". In the early twentieth century, Bertrand Russell and Maynard Keynes dreamed of a shorter working week. Hippies and punks took up the mantle in the late twentieth century. On "Seventeen" Johnny Rotten sang: "I don't work, I just speed / That's all I need" and on "Career Opportunities" Joe Strummer declared: "I won't open a letter bomb for you."

2

What Has Silicon Valley Ever Done for Us?

I'D LIKE TO SHARE with you a planned scene from a forthcoming *Idler* theatrical production about a gang of neo-Luddites plotting to overthrow the overlords of Silicon Valley.

SCENE *A meeting of the Revolutionary Idler Party.*

TOM Silicon Valley have bled us white, the bastards. They've taken everything we held dear. They've destroyed newspapers, letter-writing, childhood, musicians' incomes, teenagers' mental health, journalism, diaries, maps, day-dreaming... they've enriched themselves in the process, and what have they given us in return?

GAV The smartphone?

TOM What?

GAV The smartphone.

TOM Oh. Yeah, yeah. They did give us that. Uh, that's true. Yeah.

GAV And with Spotify you've got the world's music, right there, a click away.

IDLER 1 Yes it was terrible before. You had to pay a fortune for vinyl records. And CDs were a rip-off.

TOM All right, I'll grant you that. The smartphone and Spotify are two things Silicon Valley has done.

GAV And Zoom.

TOM Well, Zoom is great, that goes without saying. But apart from the smartphone, Spotify and Zoom …

GAV Wikipedia.

TOM All right, I grant you that, too, Wikipedia is an astounding resource.

IDLER 1 You can learn anything for free on YouTube, Tom.

IDLER 2 Accounting software is brilliant.

TOM All right, fair enough.

GAV Netflix.

IDLER 1 WhatsApp.

IDLER 2 Great home delivery.

IDLER 3 Translation devices.

TOM All right, but apart from the smartphone, Spotify, Zoom, Wikipedia, YouTube, accounting software, Netflix, WhatsApp, great home delivery and translation devices, what has Silicon Valley ever done for us?

GAV They've banished boredom.

TOM Boredom?
Oh shut up.

3
What Makes a Good Life?

AT THE HEART of what we do at the *Idler* is a continuing discussion about what makes a good life. The phrase appears first, as far as we can tell, in the utterings of Socrates. As you know, Socrates did not write anything down; what we know of him is recorded by his pupil Plato and friend Xenophon, among a few other sources.

You can compare the life of Socrates to the life of Christ, in that his teachings were about his public lectures and things he did – that is, anecdotes. These anecdotes were compiled by a later writer called Diogenes Laërtius. Philosophers then argued about the meaning of Socrates' words and actions as they developed their ideas on how to live well.

One element of the good life is to be content with little. Says Diogenes Laërtius:

Alcibiades [Socrates' rich and beautiful young friend] once offered him a large site on which to build a house; but he replied, "Suppose, then, I wanted shoes and you offered me a whole hide to make a pair with – would

it not be ridiculous in me to take it?" Often when he
looked at the multitude of wares exposed for sale,
he would say to himself, "How many things I can
do without!"

Socrates was a devotee of simple living:

He prided himself on his plain living, and never asked
a fee from anyone. He used to say that he most enjoyed
the food which was least in need of condiment, and
the drink which made him feel the least hankering for
some other drink; and that he was nearest to the gods
in that he had the fewest wants.

Socrates said that education and knowledge were intrinsic
to the good life. He enjoyed having a laugh, too:

Moreover, in his old age he learnt to play the lyre,
declaring that he saw no absurdity in learning a
new accomplishment. As Xenophon relates in the
Symposium, it was his regular habit to dance,
thinking that such exercise helped to keep the body
in good condition.

Contemplation is an essential ingredient of the good life.
In Plato's *Symposium*, Socrates talks about his visit to the
wise woman Diotima. She tells the philosopher that the
best way to live your life is to spend your time contem-

plating beauty. She says that you should start with cultural visits: "He who would proceed aright in this matter should begin in youth to visit beautiful forms." Later the philosopher moves on to the contemplation of divine beauty: "The vision is revealed to him of a single science, which is the science of beauty everywhere."

> *This, my dear Socrates, is that life above all others which man should live, in the contemplation of beauty absolute … the divine beauty, I mean, pure and clear and unalloyed, not clogged with the pollutions of mortality and all the colours and vanities of human life.*

We should add that Socrates was keen on wine. In the *Symposium*, only Socrates stays awake after the all-night drinking session and – seemingly not drunk – continues his business in Athens the morning after, while his partners in debauch are crashed out on their couches.

4
Bring Back Letter Writing

ONE OF THE many beautiful arts that Silicon Valley has killed off, in its infinite avarice, is letter-writing. Unlike emails, WhatsApp, texts and all the rest of it, letters are tactile, beautiful, individual. Every letter is different. A letter – particularly a hand-written one – oozes charm and personality. There are academics out there who are devoted to the study of Keats's letters, for example. I went to a lecture about them a few years ago. Each letter consisted of one sheet folded up into an envelope, and to save money the poet would write in the margins, using up every bit of available space.

Even in the eighties, we were still writing letters. I have a few – sweet correspondences between teenage friends, containing drawings and jokes and silly lettering.

The ancient philosophers wrote letters to each other, and in fact the progress of all human civilisation was conducted by letter until very recently. Letters had strict rules of courtesy. I remember being taught them at school. You must write "Dear X", which I found strange as "dear" seemed to me to be a very affectionate way of greeting someone you may never have met before. Then there were the sign-offs: "Yours sincerely", "Yours truly", "Yours faithfully".

There was the fun, or possibly terror, of receiving a letter. In Ivan Goncharov's novel *Oblomov*, about a lazy Russian land-owner, the generally inert Oblomov family is thrown into a state of anxiety when a letter arrives at the house. For days, they dare not open it. They stare at it, shake it, and leave it lying around, wondering what on earth could be inside it.

I find the demise of letter-writing so sad. What are future scholars going to do about the correspondence of famous writers? Will we buy books with titles like *The Collected WhatsApps of Salman Rushdie*? *The Selected Emails of Julian Barnes*? I doubt it.

That's why I'm making a new year's resolution to write more letters and postcards. I plan to start with thank-you letters, a custom which happily still survives. But having got out of the habit, writing letters doesn't seem so easy. You have to find some paper or a card. A pen that works. An envelope. You need the person's address and postcode. Then a stamp must be located (and sadly our beautiful first and second class stamps are now disfigured with a bar code of all things). Finally, you have to take the letter to a postbox. That's not easy. I tend to put the letter next to the mirror in the hall, where it says for a week. Then I put it in my jacket pocket and forget all about it. I then find it a week later when looking through my pockets for something else, but by then the letter has become sadly crumpled.

It was a slight comfort to read that this is not a new problem. In his essay "Rules for Letter Writing", Lewis Carroll has the following advice: "When you take your letters to the Post, carry them in your hand. If you put them in your pocket you will take a long country walk (I speak from experience), and passing the Post-Office twice, going and returning, and, when you get home, you will find them still in your pocket."

As for stamps, I aim to follow Nancy Mitford's delightfully snobbish advice to use second class stamps. First class stamps, she said, make you look like you're in a hurry, which is terribly vulgar. Second class stamps, then, are more idle. And they're cheaper too.

What we need to do is to get everything prepared. We need notepaper and postcards, envelopes, a pen and stamps. These should be kept together in a drawer in a desk. Thus armed, writing a postcard actually takes no time at all, and when you think of the pleasure it will bring, is well worth the effort. We occasionally receive a letter or postcard in the *Idler* office from a reader. We're always delighted and the missive goes straight onto the noticeboard. That will never happen with an email.

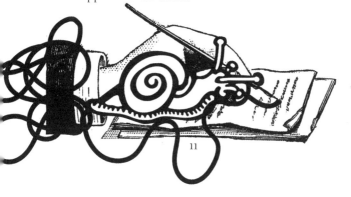

5

How to Sleep Well

THOUGH I'VE NEVER really been much good at any-thing in particular, I do have one skill of which I'm very proud, and that is sleeping. I'm really very good at it. I'm an expert dozer. I've had a talent for sleeping from a very young age. My parents called me a dormouse as I was always dropping off and found it very difficult to get out of bed in the morning. At school I would enjoy the nectar of oblivion during afternoon lessons, and teachers would whack the desk to wake me up. At my first job in journalism, I perfected a technique for napping where I would doze while cradling my head in my hands.

Most nights I sleep for nine and a half hours. In general, I go to bed at around ten, read for an hour, and wake at about 8.30am. On weekends, I lie in bed till ten or eleven.

Socrates reckoned if you wanted to do something well, you should get advice from someone who was very good at it. Hence in the *Oeconomicus*, he gets householding advice from a young man known for running an efficient household. (Socrates was suspicious of democracy, because he felt he was entrusting the running of the city to a bunch of amateurs and chancers.)

In the same spirit, I'd like to pass my sleep expertise on to you. Of course, I'm aware that some people have serious insomnia, and those I cannot help. It's one for the doctors. But here, for what it's worth, are my utterly unscientific top tips:

- Be tired in the first place. This means plenty of mental and physical exercise during the day. I cycle six to ten miles each day, and aim to play tennis three or four times a week.
- Drink lots of beer. Three pints of good ale each evening guarantees me a good night's sleep. Good beer is a sleeping draught. I'm always surprised by sleep guides that say "avoid alcohol".
- When you can't get to sleep, lie on your back staring at the ceiling, and attempt to think nice thoughts. For example, imagine friends and family smiling at you.
- Read for an hour before attempting to sleep.
- Absolutely no screens.
- Go to bed early, sometime around 10pm.
- Aim for nine hours.
- Don't be a farmer or work for Clifford Chance or Goldman Sachs.
- Be happy. Clearly stress and worry interrupt sleep.
- Avoid sleeping pills. The drugs don't work, they just make it worse.
- Absolutely no coffee after noon. Coffee hangs around in your system for eight hours or more. Author Michael Pollan calls caffeine "the enemy of good sleep". After

weaning himself off coffee, he said he "was sleeping like a teenager again".

🖐 If you can't sleep, consider doing something useful rather than worrying. When struck by insomnia, Lewis Carroll would put the light on and work on a maths problem. "I believe that an hour of calculation for me is better than an hour of worry," he said.

6

The Joy of Annoy

IT SEEMS A LOT of us spend a lot of time being annoyed. We enjoy it. This pleasure in getting peeved was not recommended by the Stoic philosophers. They reckoned you should treat annoyances with great equanimity, and this attitude is summed up by a little comedy routine I once saw. The comic came on stage wearing a toga and declared himself to be a Stoic stand-up. And his first joke went like this: "You know what really annoys me?" he asked the audience. "Nothing!"

Sometimes the word "annoying" is used completely witlessly, as when commentators of the Rod Liddle variety describe someone with whom they disagree (say, Greta Thunberg) as "annoying", which is an amazingly unsophisticated and childish sort of insult. I find that really annoying.

The point about annoyance, though, is that sometimes your annoyance is justified, and occasionally you do something about it, something positive. It used to annoy me that teenagers studying A Level English were unable to put the apostrophe in the right place. So I helped to launch the

Bad Grammar Award, which attempted to teach people the rudiments of good punctuation. The Sex Pistols found the society of the 1970s extremely annoying and their annoyance resulted in one of the best LPs ever made. William Cobbett was superb at being annoyed (he was a "good hater") and one of his annoyances – that people of the early 19th century had forgotten how to bake bread – led to him producing an excellent guide to self-sufficiency called *Cottage Economy*.

Cobbett was also very annoyed by the insults and hatred directed towards the Luddite protestors, whom he saw as being justified in their annoyance at the new machinery:

> *The abuse which has been heaped upon you by those base writers whose object is to inflame one part of the people against the other; the horrid stories which have been retailed about your injustice and cruelty; the murderous punishments which these writers express their wish to see inflicted on you; the delight which they evidently feel when any of you come to an untimely end; all these produce no feeling in my mind other than that of abhorrence of your calumniators.*

7
On Being Hungover

N OW THIS IS A subject on which, I flatter myself, I am something of an expert. This morning I'm suffering from a hangover caused by merry-making for our *Thirty Years of the Idler* book launch at Rough Trade East last night. After the party a few of us carried on drinking at the bar next door, then later sat round our kitchen table with more beer till two in the morning.

It's not the worst hangover I've ever had. I'm not in enormous pain. I haven't needed a painkiller. But there is a palpable slowness to my thinking and writing speed. I'm reminded of a great song called "Hungover at Mass" by Irish songwriter Junior Brother (who I saw play last weekend at a great festival called Other Voices on the west coast of Ireland). In this anguished tune the writer worries that the devil got into him on the previous night. "Does God want me embarrassed?" he wonders. "Does Jesus have me cursed?" Strange things happen to his perception: "I feel everyone's eyes, even the baby Jesus statue comes alive."

It's true that hangovers can take on a spiritual quality in that they take you to a different dimension, where sounds are louder and objects wobble. Zen writer Shunryu Suzuki certainly believed so. "I think you do not feel so well. Your mind is full of 'weeds'. But if you can cease striving to overcome those weeds, they, too, can enrich your path to enlightenment." My friend Josh Glenn commented: "The hangover can propel us into a 'middle state' of perceptivity quite unlike anything we're ever likely to experience outside a monastery."

Rupert Sheldrake has written a book about various methods of "going beyond", including festivals, sports and psychedelics. Maybe he should add the hangover to this list?

Hangovers, it's true, don't go well with childcare or work in general (although I know writers who are happy to write with a hangover). And I'm acutely aware in my own case that a hangover can tend to make me a bit short-tempered. Therefore it's probably a good idea to plan a day of serious idling the day after a party. And to keep my mouth shut when I feel a sharp comment bubbling up.

Socrates didn't seem to suffer from hangovers. At the end of the *Symposium*, after drinking all night, he steps over sleeping revellers and walks into the street: "First Aristophanes dropped into a slumber, and then, as day began to dawn, Agathon also. When Socrates had seen them comfortable, he rose and went away…on arriving at the Lyceum, he washed himself, and then spent the rest of the day in his ordinary fashion; and so, when the day was done, he went home for the evening and reposed."

8

On Being Unnecessary

WE WERE IN the kitchen with my seventeen-year-old son. I mentioned to him that Victoria and I were thinking of going away for a couple of days. Would he be OK on his own, we asked.

"Er, yes?" he said, looking at us as if we were creatures of much lower than average intelligence, and then added: "You're unnecessary."

As I cycled to the *Idler* office, I pondered the feeling of being "unnecessary". The word is at first glance faintly insulting. It punctures my inflated sense of self-importance. I am surplus to requirements, redundant, useless, unimportant, no longer needed.

But to be unnecessary is in fact liberating and strangely pleasurable. For one thing, I hope it means we've done a reasonable job of bringing up this child. The aim of parenting should be to produce a cheerful, self-sufficient adult, one who can tie his own bootlaces, wash his own clothes, cook his own meals, do his homework without being nagged and yes, find his parents to be unnecessary.

Maybe being unnecessary also means I can now be more

footloose and fancy free, as I was in my twenties. Being unnecessary means no one cares what I do, and nor do I. Unnecessariness means freedom.

There's something satisfyingly Taoist about becoming unnecessary. The Taoist sage, after all, does very little. "Do that which consists in taking no action," says Lao Tzu, "and order will prevail." The sage also advises: "Withdraw when work is done."

And self-importance is very dangerous, as Bertrand Russell commented: "One of the symptoms of an impending nervous breakdown is the belief that one's work is terribly important." And while we're quoting the great *Idler* elders, let's not forget that determinedly Taoist prophet Oscar Wilde, who said: "Action is the refuge of people who have nothing whatsoever to do."

We're told that magic mushrooms are good for your mental health because they destroy the ego. Well if you have children, you clearly have no need for magic mushrooms.

9

How Dreaming Can Cure Envy

Envy is an emotion that spares few of us, even the most talented and successful. I remember seeing an interview with David Bowie where he confessed to it. He said he was envious of Bob Dylan's prodigious output. "I heard, and I was green with envy, Dylan's got a hundred and forty songs he chooses from for a setlist." Bowie at this stage had a mere fifty.

In my case I often get a pang of envy when walking past a bookshop. Why is one of my books not in the window? How come they're stocking the *Paris Review* and not the *Idler*? Grrr! I sometimes find myself avoiding bookshops for this reason. At other times I find myself being momentarily and irrationally envious of someone who works in a completely different field – an actor, say (especially if they went to my school), despite the fact that I know absolutely nothing about their everyday life and have no desire to be an actor.

The great Dr Johnson was enormously successful yet he

wasn't immune from the snares of envy. He reckoned it was part and parcel of being a writer. In his poem "The Vanity of Human Wishes" he wrote:

Mark what ills the scholar's life assail,
Toil, envy, want, the garret and the jail.

Which is a pretty gloomy assessment of the writer's life, though largely true. However, Johnson reckoned you could banish envy with a simple trick. In one of his "Idler" columns, he made the comforting assertion: "All envy would be extinguished, if it were universally known that there are none to be envied." Everyone's got their problems and stresses.

In the same piece, Dr Johnson recommended two different cures for melancholy musing. One was solitude, and the other was company. Though at first these seem diametrically opposed, he argues that in fact they offer the same thing – a refuge in dreams: "Many have no happier moments than those that they pass in solitude, abandoned to their own imagination," he writes.

I discovered this week that Delia Smith is a convert to this way of thinking. In a new book she promotes the idea that everyone should spend an hour a day occupied in what she calls "reflective daydreaming". Well done, Delia!

But there are those other people, says Dr Johnson, who crave the fellowship of other human beings to distract them from their woes: "Others are afraid to be alone, and amuse themselves by a perpetual succession of companions." Dr Johnson himself fell into this latter camp.

He argues that the end result is the same: "in solitude we have our dreams to ourselves, and in company we agree to dream in concert. The end sought in both is forgetfulness of ourselves."

10

On Being Ill

VICTORIA HAD TESTED positive for Covid and had been bed-bound, so it was only a matter of time, I suppose, before I'd get it. I started feeling ill last Sunday – fluey – and went to bed, and there I have remained for five days now.

I'm not feeling sorry for myself. Not at all. The light level of illness I've got has much to recommend it, particularly for idlers or those of us who aspire to more idling. I mean, yes, you have to put up with the symptoms – coughing, spluttering, weird aches, the occasional pain in the eyeballs – but putting that aside, being ill, for me anyway, has been a gift. Over the last five days I've daydreamed, caught up with my diary-writing, eaten huge amounts of fruit, taken two-hour naps after breakfast, spent no money, had a break from drinking, stared out of the window, watched *Peaky Blinders* in bed on the laptop and cancelled all appointments. I've enjoyed the delicious sensation of a suspension of responsibility. Being ill can be a holiday from the existential burden of carrying the world's weight on your shoulders.

But perhaps the greatest of the luxuries afforded by being bed-bound has been re-reading Sherlock Holmes. Over the last few days I've delighted in *The Memoirs of Sherlock Holmes*, *A Study in Scarlet*, and *The Valley of Fear*. All pure joy. It's nice, for one thing, to be reminded that Holmes is an idler. In fact, idling is at the heart of his methods. He needs to think. Like Dr Johnson, he vacillates between hyperactivity and total lethargy. Watson tells us:

The outbursts of passionate energy when he performed the remarkable feats with which his name is associated were followed by reactions of lethargy, during which he would lie about with his violin and his books, hardly moving, save from the sofa to the table.

Unlike Dr Johnson though, Holmes never feels guilty about doing nothing. "I'm the most incurably lazy fellow who ever stood in shoe leather," he boasts. Nor, it would appear, does taking class A drugs trouble his conscience. And this is a habit which even strait-laced Dr Watson doesn't seem to think is particularly reprehensible: "Save for the occasional use of cocaine, he had no vices."

What has surprised me on this rereading is that Watson is also an idler – when he's not springing from his chair in amazement at one of Holmes's feats of deduction, that is. When the two first meet as young men, and agree to take rooms together, they outline to each other their shortcomings. Holmes says he gets down in the dumps, plays the violin and smokes tobacco. Watson, just back from the war in Afghanistan, and clearly suffering from PTSD, says, "I keep a bull-pup. I object to rows because my nerves are shaken, and I get up at all sorts of ungodly hours, and I am extremely lazy."

I'd also forgotten that large sections of the books read like Tarantino-esque Westerns. The second part of *The Valley of Fear* is set in a lawless mining town in the States and is horribly violent. There's one awful scene where the elderly editor of the local newspaper is beaten nearly to death by thugs.

And in *A Study in Scarlet*, you can hear the Ennio Morricone music in the background as Conan Doyle tells the tale of a troop of Mormons rescuing a dying man and young girl in the desert, while on their way to establish their polygamous utopia in Salt Lake City.

But we always return, after the action, to the comforting cocoon of 221B Baker Street, to conviviality and interesting work, and freedom, and sitting around doing nothing.

11

Make Work into Play

A LOVELY LINE from Alan Watts has been going round my head over the last couple of weeks: "This is the real secret of life – to be completely engaged with what you are doing in the here and now. And instead of calling it work, realise it is play."

Paul McCartney expressed a similar sentiment. When recording, he said the Beatles would joke that they'd put in a hard day's play. They were mucking about, being silly, being in the moment.

It's a great state of mind to get yourself into. Suddenly acres of pleasure and happiness open out to you. Think of each day as a succession of small joys. Sleep, sunshine, cycling through the city, the pub, interesting and enjoyable work for the lucky ones, reading, a shower, beer, coffee, eggs, a delicious nap, a cheese sandwich, sitting on a bench, staring into space, playing tennis, talking to your spouse or children or friends. Whatever it is that you find yourself doing, enjoy it.

Even the duties and the things you don't really want to do can be a source of happiness or at least fascination. I would rather not have to go to the supermarket (and at one stage in my life I managed to boycott them). Or the motorway service station. But actually, look at all the life there, the people, the things, the wonderful bazaar of ingredients. Doing the dishes can be fun: enjoy the warm water, and derive satisfaction, as Geoff Dyer does, in creating a tottering pile of clean pots and pans in the drainer. DH Lawrence loved cleaning. For him it was a creative act. And he did it well. "If Lawrence swept the floor," said Aldous Huxley, "the floor was swept." (I have tried to apply this cheerful philosophy to picking up my dog's poo in a small plastic bag and putting it in a bin on the city streets, but I confess failure on that one.)

And Watts's idea of life as play has much in common with the Eastern mystical idea of detachment, which we could also call, "not taking things too seriously". Laughing at your misfortunes. Understanding that you are playing a role, that you're an actor, that all the world's a stage.

The musical accompaniment to such reflections for me has been a lovely song called "The Drum". The version I like is a cover of the original, which was a strange ditty by Slapp Happy, the avant-garde music project of Peter Blegvad. The band who did the cover version are called Bongwater and they were a cult success in the late eighties and early nineties. They comprised the musical genius Kramer and the multi-talented writer and performer Ann Magnuson. Bongwater's version samples the wise utterances of an unknown American sage who declares: "The key is now. This is the moment in which we can do: now. What we call the future is man's hope of the future, what he is hoping, now."

So thinking about the future (and the past), which some self-help gurus warn against, is actually another form of being in the present. Taking trips down memory lane or conjuring up visions of future projects are themselves great pleasures.

12

Be an OOOFER

YOU MAY HAVE had a similar conversation recently, about offices and office life. I've lost count of the number of people I've heard say, over the last few months, "I never want to go back to the office again."

This trend is partly a result of the pandemic, but it's also a demographic thing. I suppose I'm mainly talking about people in their fifties. Some of them had had enough before the pandemic and were already making sounds about breaking free. Others have found a new sense of autonomy as a result of working from home during lockdowns, and are unwilling to give it up.

While on holiday this summer I met several such people. They'd worked out that they could leave Blighty over the summer for far longer than the standard two weeks holiday offered by the previous system. With laptops, they could combine work and holiday and be away for a few weeks.

Victoria and I did something similar: we spent four weeks in a flat in Croatia, and I was able to get the magazine sent off to the printer from our Dalmatian retreat. A bit of work in the morning followed by lunch, siesta, swim and dinner.

Not bad. It's the kind of life that I believe Graham Greene led: a sort of permanent holiday punctuated by bursts of work. Greene, I remember hearing from someone who knew him well, worked every day from eight till 11am, generally in the south of France, then had his first cocktail.

Anyway it's a trend to be welcomed and I have a name for these new freedom-seekers: they are the OOOFERs. This acronym, of my own invention, stands for Out Of Office For Ever. Related to OOOFERs is another idea, which is: "things that make you go OOO", and this refers to fun activities that get you out of the office. "Picking your children up from university" is a good example of an OOO. Victoria recently did this, spending a pleasant day away from work by driving to Bristol to collect our daughter, and enjoying lunch in a trendy Mediterranean eaterie in Clifton.

For my part, I'm not an OOOFER. I love the mix of home work and office work. We've now had the same office for six years and it's been a lifeline. It's like a shed, a refuge, a space of freedom. It's under the Westway so I think about The Clash nearly every day. It provides me with a lovely cycle ride along the Great Western Canal and across Portobello Road. And I think of it as a studio. Like a band, it's fun to work in a group in real life together some days. Doing a nine-to-five can be enjoyable, creative, productive. Free-flowing chat leads to ideas.

Other days, it's nice to stay at home.

13

Just Don't Do It

W E'RE ALWAYS hearing about the importance of
making to-do lists. "Be productive. Make a to-do list."
I make them myself all the time, I admit. For freelancers,
the to-do list is a way of internalising the boss. It's a bit like
that expression, "I'm my own boss". Perhaps because we are
afraid of not having a boss, we create an inner boss, or what
Bruce Robinson calls the "government of the mind", and
use that inner finger-wagger to wield power over our inner
shirker. With the to-do list, we split ourselves in two, master
and slave.

We also automatically make ourselves feel inadequate
because the to-do list is inevitably too ambitious. *To do: Get
milk. Iron shirt. Write novel. Solve the world's most pressing problems. Reverse climate change. Be the best version of
myself I can be.* It's the inescapable fate of a to-do list to be
left tragically uncompleted. (When and if you do make a
to-do list, then do keep it short.)

Much like Nike's slogan "Just Do It" (just do what?),
the to-do list feeds into the myth that any sort of activity is
better than inactivity. That's clearly nonsense. Hitler was

highly active but it would have been better for the world if he'd stayed at home and stuck to his painting.

Don't you think, then, as an antidote to excessive activity, it would be a good idea to get into the habit of creating a "do not" list? Because, as Lin Yutang says, we should cultivate the noble art of leaving things undone, of not interfering, of just not bothering. How about not driving a car, not starting a war, not getting an aeroplane, not flying to the moon, not posting on Instagram, not starting a YouTube channel, not responding to a Tweet, not creating a lot of unnecessary fuss and work and using up oil in the process? Not doing things, as I am fond of pointing out, will save the planet, since it is activity which uses up energy. Lying on your back on the floor or in bed or in the park with a book uses no oil.

What would be on your "do not" list? Here are some suggestions:

Do not … get up.
Do not … buy a new car on hire purchase.
Do not … put your clothes in the tumble dryer.
Do not … invade Ukraine.
Do not … iron shirts.
Do not … buy a gun.
Do not … buy Twitter.
Do not … criticise your partner.
Do not … scrap the 45p top rate of income tax and replace it with a 40p rate.

Do not … peel potatoes.
Do not … watch *Game of Thrones*.
Do not … buy Bitcoin.
Do not … listen to the *Today* programme.
Do not … worry about things you can't control.

14
Go to Bed Early

I DON'T KNOW about you, but these days I derive huge joy from going to bed early. On climbing into bed at nine with a herbal tea and a book on Greek philosophy, I can be heard through the house making an irritating exhalation of pure pleasure. "Ah! This is amazing!"

Of course, it wasn't always this way. In my hedonistic twenties, I didn't think I'd had a proper night out if it didn't involve ingesting a cocktail of mind-bending drugs and staying up till dawn or later. Once or twice a week I'd have a "quiet night in" but this was sometimes a bit of an effort and really only done in order to recover sufficiently to go out again. "As they pulled you out of the oxygen tent, you asked for the latest party," as David Bowie put it on 1974's "Diamond Dogs".

But as that other genius Bryan Ferry put it, in the same year, on "Mother of Pearl": "Well I've been up all night, party-time wasting, it's too much fun." Much better to go to bed early and reflect on life's inner meaning for an hour before drifting off into a dreamy sleep.

You may even get to experience the same sort of hyper-sophisticated literary sleep that Proust described in *Swann's Way*. As you may remember, for a long time, he went to bed early. "*Longtemps, je me suis couché de bonne heure.*" Note the French word for early is "good". The literal translation would be something like, "Long time, I laid myself down of good hour."

As he read, he would nod off, and then start to dream:

I had been thinking all the time, while I was asleep, of what I had just been reading, but my thoughts had run into a channel of their own, until I myself seemed actually to have become the subject of my book: a church, a quartet, the rivalry between François I and Charles V.

There you go: you could actually be a church! Proust also savours the sensual joy of being in bed: "I would lay my cheeks gently against the comfortable cheeks of my pillow, as plump and blooming as the cheeks of babyhood." Ah, sweet little Marcel! (We understand that while confined to his bed in this way, he indulged in the early twentieth century equivalent of Deliveroo: his housekeeper Céleste Albaret would order takeouts for him from Paris's finest hotels. Lucky Proust.)

Going to bed early is surely also good for your health. We hear a lot about the problem of sleep, of insomnia, and indeed there are even apps which turn sleep into a sort of competitive sport and claim to get you the right amount of it. Which reminds me of Bertie Wooster's ruminations on sleep science: "One of the Georges – I forget which – once said that a certain number of hours' sleep each night – I cannot recall at the moment how many – made a man something which for the time being has slipped my memory."

People would find there's no need for these sleep apps if they knew the simple trick which is to get into bed at nine with a book and without a phone. There should be no computer in the room either, nothing which digitally connects you to the world out there and makes you "available". This is a time for you.

I think television isn't much of a help. Too often in lockdown, Victoria and I would watch three episodes of some horrifyingly violent drama and then go to bed after midnight, our brains teeming with images of blood and gore. Not good for the old shut-eye.

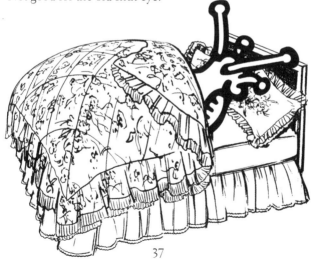

15

Whatever Happened to Elevenses?

WHEN I WAS growing up my Dad used to love elevenses. It was an important custom to him. At 11am, during the holidays, we stopped whatever we were doing and with great joy he would set out a little treat for my brother and me. Sometimes it was biscuits, sometimes a Tunnock's caramel wafer, and sometimes he made banana sandwiches on brown bread. He mashed up the bananas with a lot of sugar. I imagine he had a cup of tea with this little feast.

"Elevenses, elevenses!" he would say, grinning and clearly relishing the sound of the word itself. There's something comical in it, isn't there? It sounds almost like a baby word, like an affectionate nickname.

Even today, though he is now over 80 and lives an ascetic lifestyle on a meditation retreat near Oxford, he still loves stuffing his face with biscuits at eleven, or, more likely, ten to.

Elevenses, like afternoon tea, is a little detour in the day, a break from toil. The word, or something similar to it, appears in the OED as a bit of Suffolk dialect from 1849. The entry also mentions "fours": "RAYNBIRD Agric. Suffolk vi. 296 The name 'fourzes' and 'elevens', given to these short periods of rest and refreshment, show when taken." Food historian Alan Davidson reckons the word first appeared in the eighteenth century.

So, like the tea break, it's certainly been around since the Industrial Revolution, but surely the custom is ancient? I can imagine shepherds in Roman times resting under a tree after a hard morning's herding, and getting out a little cake to scoff.

Eleven o'clock feels like a very natural time for a rest. When I lived in the countryside and wrote books full-time, I made sure that on the dot of eleven I got up from my desk, walked into the kitchen and made myself a little "smack-erel" of something, to use Winnie the Pooh's expression. Pooh's clock, you will remember, "stopped at five minutes to eleven some weeks ago," meaning that the idle bear is blissfully trapped in a sort of eternal elevenses. In philo-sophical mood, Pooh comforts his readers thus: "When late morning rolls around, and you're feeling a bit out of sorts, don't worry; you're probably just a little eleven o'clockish." That's the time for some bread and honey.

That other literary and idle bear, Paddington, takes elev-enses with Mr Gruber in his antique shop. Buns and hot chocolate were their choice of snack.

Tolkien says the hobbits loved elevenses, and one of the

Lord of the Rings films has this delightful little exchange. The hobbits are on a trek when hobbit Pippin suggests they take a break. The hard-working human Aragorn is all for pressing on:

ARAGORN: *Gentlemen, we do not stop till nightfall.*
PIPPIN: *What about breakfast?*
MERRY: *You've already had it.*
PIPPIN: *We've had one, yes. What about second breakfast?*
MERRY: *Don't think he knows about second breakfast, Pip.*
PIPPIN: *What about elevenses? Luncheon? Afternoon tea? Dinner? Supper? He knows about them, doesn't he?*
MERRY: *I wouldn't count on it.*

"Second breakfast" is a good name for elevenses, and indeed the Polish custom of taking a mid-morning break, and snack, probably a sausage, is called exactly that: *drugie śniadanie*.

Personally speaking, I take elevenses most Sunday mornings, after a tennis game. The four of us repair to a café after our match and indulge in coffee and a ham and cheese croissant, which is a hearty second breakfast indeed (my first breakfast generally consists of a poached egg with toast followed by a second slice of toast with marmalade). Though I think elevenses properly understood should consist of a sweet snack and tea, not coffee.

I'll let Tolkien have the last words on the subject: "If more of us valued food and cheer and song above hoarded gold, it would be a merrier world."

16

Turn off the News; Turn on Radio 3

A FEW WEEKS AGO Victoria turned off Radio 4 in the morning. Instead she turned on Radio 3. And she says her mood has soared ever since. Radio 4, and the *Today* programme in particular, seem expressly designed to make you angry about matters over which you have absolutely no control. The news, as Morrissey pointed out, tries to frighten you, to make you feel small and alone. Discussion programmes are all about arguing. They may be entertaining, in the same way as watching gladiators was entertaining. But they're hardly edifying and certainly not transcendent.

Radio 3, on the other hand, lifts you up to other-wordly planes. Here is the world's most beautiful music, chosen by lovely knowledgeable presenters, emerging for free from the radio in the corner of the room. It's a blessing, nay, a miracle. It's a spiritual experience.

Your companions on weekday mornings are Petroc Trelawny and Georgia Mann, both very amiable hosts. There's a little bit of news, so you don't feel completely out of touch. But very little.

We now just leave the radio on all day, so whenever you walk into the kitchen, you will hear Vivaldi (the Composer of the Week) or Bach or something more obscure. Think how miraculous the people of the eighteenth century would have found the wireless: an entire invisible orchestra playing for you!

Radio 3 is experimental too and never afraid of the avant garde, as any listener to *Night Tracks* will attest. You can hear some really weird sounds coming out of the radio late at night.

Then there's their brilliant words and music strand, where seemingly random bits of poetry and prose are read by actors and interspersed with relevant music. There's no commentary or explanation. It's like a work of audio art. It's called simply *Words and Music* and goes out on Sundays at 5.30pm.

And then there's my favourite of all, *The Early Music Show* on Sundays at 2pm, when the presenters go back to medieval, Renaissance and Baroque periods. Lutes, harpsichords and viola da gambas galore.

Now these presenters – what a great job they have! I can't think of a more idle occupation than "Radio 3 DJ". The job involves only the tiniest bit of chat: "That was a lovely recording of Mozart's Violin Concerto No.5 in A Major with Arthur Grumiaux and the London Symphony Orchestra conducted there by Sir Colin Davis." Then you just press a button and drift off for another twenty minutes. And the show lasts only two or three hours. Nice work if you can get it.

It's the anti-work radio station. While Zoe Ball and Chris Evans are all about cheering up and distracting the workers for a day of picking and packing in the warehouse, Radio 3 takes you to sublime worlds which make you question the need for work at all.

Some of the titles of the shows, it's true, strike a bum note. *Music Matters* must be the worst name ever for a programme about music. And some are sweetly innocent and 1950s-sounding: *In Tune*, for example. Though this is an excellent show where Sean Rafferty interviews young stars of classical music.

Radio 3's listening figures are not massive. Radio 2 gets nearly 15 million listeners a week. Radio 4 nearly ten million. 6 Music (also great) gets 2.5 million, and Radio 3 gets two million. Still, that's an awful lot of people.

Truly, I repeat, Radio 3 is a blessing from the gods, and I beseech the poets to compose an ode in Latin to its joys.

17
On Being Annoying

W E'RE ALL AWARE of philosophical tracts and essays which start with the word "on". Montaigne was the master of these. "On Sleep", "On Names", "On Thumbs" and "On a Monstrous Child" are a few examples. The "on" is sometimes translated as "of" and that's because the Latin word "De" is used in essay titles, as in "De Profundis" by Oscar Wilde.

Renaissance essays and tracts often used the "de" word. There's a very successful heavy metal band which gets its name from a 1556 book called *De Re Metallica*, meaning "on metallic things".

There's also a farming guidebook by Columella, who lived around 70BC, called *De Re Rustica*. This gave me the idea of starting a folk band with heavy metal influences called Rustica, but I couldn't convince anyone else of the brilliance of this scheme. I did however use a lot of Columella's quotes as source material for my slightly strange husbandry manual, *Brave Old World* (now retitled *How to Live in the Country*, in a futile attempt to get more sales).

This philosophical naming custom seems to originate with the ancient Greeks. A good proportion of Aristotle's essays begin with "on". We have "On Memory", "On Sleep", "On Virtues and Vices" and the lovely "On Marvellous Things Heard".

The literary shrink Adam Phillips played with this idea with his wittily titled collection, *On Tickling, Kissing and Being Bored*. And Virginia Woolf wrote an essay called "On Being Ill".

But among all these "ons" and "ofs" I don't remember ever reading a philosophical tract called "On Being Annoying". This is strange because if there's one besetting sin of philosophers and writers and artists of all sorts, it's that they're really irritating. Socrates was so annoying that the Athenians voted to have him executed. His wife Xanthippe found him totally infuriating. He was always philosophising, and flirting with Alcibiades, and never earning any money. She supposedly tipped a chamber pot over his head in her fury at his annoying ways, a scene that became a favourite subject for Renaissance artists, and was celebrated by Chaucer's Wife of Bath.

And Socrates referred to himself as the "gadfly of Athens". That shows wisdom and self-knowledge. I notice, speaking personally, that though I find other people really annoying, all the time, it rarely occurs to me that they might find me annoying. In my own mind, I'm a perfectly rational and considerate being who never irritates anyone else.

My children, thankfully, are quick to disabuse me of my

self-delusion. "You're so ANNOYING!" shouts my daughter when I persist in arguing a point beyond the level of endurance, or when I interrupt, or when I talk about myself incessantly, or when I know better than everyone else, or when I repeat the same old boring opinion or the same old boring anecdote for the millionth time, or do something else really annoying.

I suppose that, seen from a certain angle, annoyingness can be good. Gandhi was really annoying. He annoyed Churchill. "It is alarming and nauseating to see Mr Gandhi, a seditious Middle Temple lawyer, now posing as a fakir … striding half-naked up the steps of the Vice-regal Palace." But Gandhi liberated India. And the Suffragettes were annoying. They were terrorists. They caused all kinds of upset. But their irritating tactics and persistence worked.

I confess to being annoying when pursuing well-known people for interviews or to write articles in the *Idler*. But I do it because I think the magazine will benefit.

So I suppose in this proposed essay, I could distinguish between "good annoying" and "bad annoying", since if the people annoyed are the oppressors, then that's "good annoying". Or if the annoyingness leads to an artistic creation that people enjoy, that's also good annoying. But if the people annoyed are one's own friends and family members (as is the case with me), then that's "bad annoying".

18

A Manifesto for Slow Learning

Towards the end of last year I travelled to Turin for an all-day symposium at the UN's International Labour Organization training centre. The subject was "Slow Education". We've had "slow food", the thinking went. How about applying the principles of slowness to education? Could we outline a philosophy, and start a movement?

Around fifteen of us – authors, artists, teachers – spent the day chatting and playing with coloured marker pens and large pieces of paper, and by the end of the day we'd come up with what we called a "Bill of Rights", ten manifesto points for slow learners.

I think the ten points are pretty good reminders for all of us of the pressing need to slow down. They're also very "*Idler*", and I'm quietly pleased that idling principles are making their way into such an important and global institution.

So here are the ten points with a bit of explanation for each. I guess they were developed mainly with adult training in mind. However, I think they could be applied to any educational situation, whether it's school or university or one of you doing an Idler online course.

As a bill of rights, each item on the list is preceded by the statement: "You have a right to …"

1. Focus on direction, not destination
   Immerse yourself completely in the journey and you will reach your final goal gradually.

2. Raise your hand
   Asking questions is a fundamental human right.

3. Learn at your own pace
   Find your rhythm, find your flow. Don't compare yourself to others.

4. Unplug
   You have the right to disconnect and move your attention towards what's essential. Learn unplugged, far away from digital distractions.

5. Change your learning path (and mind)
   Don't get too comfortable in the habit zone and start with changing the aversion to change. Think differently and learn new things.

6. Take a break
   Micro-breaks, lunch breaks, and longer breaks will all improve your learning performance. You have the right to rest.

7. Make mistakes
   Don't fall into despair but Fail Forward.

8. Leave it unfinished
   We live in a super busy, multi-tasking, results-oriented society. Step away from your long to-do list and enjoy once in a while the beauty of an unstructured day.

9. Unlearn and forget
   Harness the power of unlearning. Reboot your mind, abandon old knowledge, actions and behaviours to create space.

10. Slow down
    Sometimes slow and steady will win the learning race. Make haste slowly.

This all seems to me to be eminently sensible. The points recall Socrates and the Athenian philosophers, who really did take their time. Aristotle studied for twenty years under Plato before going off to start his own school, and they all enjoyed teaching in olive groves and under trees in an unhurried manner.

One point I made at the symposium is that for the ancient Greeks, learning and leisure were precisely the same thing. The Greek word *skole*, which eventually turned into our word "school", means "leisure" or "free time". Education should be fun and it should be a lifelong process, not merely a means to getting a job, i.e. earning money.

19

How Quickly Should You Reply to Emails?

SOMETIMES, WHEN I answer emails quickly, which I always try to, people say: "That's not very idle!" They think, reasonably enough, that being idle is synonymous with being inefficient, slack and slow.

When the ultimate idler, Oblomov (in Ivan Goncharov's novel of the same name), received a letter, he would look at it for days before opening it. And the sender would be lucky to get a reply within a year, as I recall.

I have friends who deliberately take a long time to reply to an email, or don't answer at all, with the idea that people will eventually stop sending them emails, resulting in a slimmer inbox. If you answer them quickly, the argument goes, you'll get more of them. Ignore them, on the other hand, and they'll go away.

But surely it could be argued that getting back to your correspondents quickly is a very good idea as far as idling goes and that in fact, efficiency and idling are closely related. First off, a swift response is nice for the other person. They know their message has been received. It's also good for your own head. Your mind doesn't get filled up with "things to do", replies to send, that hovering sense of guilt and worry. There's less stuff hanging over you. Furthermore, you'll avoid the chase-up email from your correspondent, resulting in less work for you. Despatch business swiftly, and your burden will lighten.

It's very satisfying, as well, looking at that little envelope sign and seeing that there are zero emails to check. Sometimes I glance over someone else's shoulder at their screen and see an unimaginably huge number – like 23,465 – next to their little envelope. Surely that weighs on them at some level?

Finally, I'd argue that if you get your work done at great speed, then that will leave more time for sitting in the pub or staring out of the window or going for a long walk.

Truly, efficiency leads to idling.

20

Aldous Huxley's Intense Dislike of Work

ALDOUS HUXLEY was no fan of work. While preparing for a talk this week on the novelist, essayist and mystical explorer (he invented the word "psychedelic"), I came across several references to his desire to avoid honest toil.

Born in 1894, Huxley – who is most famous of course for *Brave New World* – shot to fame in his twenties with brilliant witty novels like *Crome Yellow*. Around the time he declared: "Like every man of sense and good feeling, I abominate work."

He got a job reviewing books for *Vogue* in London, which sounds like a nice gig, but complained to his father: "I moulder along in a pretty chronic state of boredom, and my dislike of work grows steadily towards a fanatical passion."

Later he wrote: "On the whole I am fairly happy, but I have decided that God never intended me to do any regular work."

His whole career then, like the careers of many writers

and artists and musicians, could be seen as one long attempt to escape from work.

In his novel *Antic Hay* the main protagonist, an Eton schoolmaster, reflects his creator's views: "Work, thought Gumbril, Lord, how passionately he disliked work!" In order to avoid this curse, Gumbril dreams up a new invention, pneumatic trousers, designed to be inflated when the bottom finds itself sitting on an uncomfortable surface like wood or stone. Gumbril reckons his inflatable pants will be an enormous financial success and liberate him from toil.

For his own part, Huxley never lost hope for a similar windfall. Like many writers and essentially lazy people, he considered that a massive financial success would free him from the need to pump out the books, journalism and film scripts that provided his income. To that end he wrote plays with the hope of a big West End smash, but this never happened.

Work for him was a kind of slavery to the machine. "Rigorously practised for a few generations, this dreadful religion of the machine will end by destroying the human race." Like another great English mystic, Blake, he personified the military-industrial complex as "Moloch", a god from the Old Testament who apparently demanded child sacrifice. The machine provided distraction and pleasure but held most of us in a state of slavery.

Politically we would probably call him a "philosophic anarchist". His own positive ideas for humanity to escape the grip of Moloch were things like small self-sufficient communities, à la Kropotkin. He also, of course, promoted a mystical consciousness, prefiguring the new age movement. For him mysticism was the common ground among religions, and his book *The Perennial Philosophy* is a handy primer of mystical writings which shows that Christian mystics, Islamic mystics, Buddhist mystics, Hindu mystics, Taoist mystics and all the rest are saying the same thing: be here now. "Mysticism has the enormous merit of being concerned with the eternal present, and not, as humanism is, with the future."

His last novel, *Island*, is an attempt to outline a more or less ideal society (Frank Kermode said "it must be one of the worst novels ever written" because it's more of a political manifesto than a story populated by believable characters).

I think Huxley would approve of Idler principles.

21

Baths versus Showers

IN MARCH 2023, I took a trip to New York and found it to be no place for an idler. Of course there's the dashing about, the sirens, the fury, the aggression, the soup lines and the sad, sad people you see on the streets, the crazies, broken people pushing shopping trolleys, often with a great sense of purpose, as if they're still hanging on to the American dream.

But there's also the lack of baths. There are only showers, at least where I stayed. And this reminded me of a letter I recently received on the subject from the great Simon Fairlie, Cobbettesque champion of small farmers, magazine editor, seller of scythes, maker of cheese and keeper of pigs:

Nearly fifty years ago, a certain writer praised baths. "Turning the tap with one's toes," he wrote, "is the mark of the true bather, and few sensations are more pleasurable than, when one's bath has become a little tepid, feeling the new hot water slowly lap up one's body and once again one is wrapped in it." The writer in question, who happened to be my father, went on to explain that he did not encounter the shower until he first visited America. He reckoned Americans' incessant showering had a lot to do with their being "always on the go, never able to take things quietly", leading them to seek compensation through self-actualization thera- pies and the like. "Only a nation that showers instead of taking baths would have to pay money to be taught how to meditate and relax."

Sylvia Plath was another literary bath fan. "There must be quite a few things a hot bath won't cure, but I don't know many of them," she said, famously. "Whenever I'm sad I'm going to die, or so nervous I can't sleep, or in love with somebody I won't be seeing for a week, I slump down just so far and then I say: 'I'll go take a hot bath.'"

Baths were big in the Middle Ages. A fifteenth-century writer on household matters offers tips for servants on how to prepare the ideal bath for the master. It all sounds a bit like a wellness ritual from the head of Gwyneth Paltrow:

Hang sheets, round the roof, every one full of flowers and sweet green herbs, and have five or six sponges to sit or lean upon, and see that you have one big sponge to sit upon, and a sheet over so that he may bathe there for a while, and have a sponge also for under his feet, if there be any to spare, and always be careful that the door is shut. Have a basin full of hot fresh herbs and

wash his body with a soft sponge, rinse him with fair
warm rose-water, and throw it over him.

In medieval cities, public bathhouses, of which there were many, doubled up as restaurants and sex retreats. Historian Virginia Smith, in her book *Clean: A History of Personal Hygiene and Purity*, says couples and groups had baths together and were served food while sitting in the water:

> *Bath feasting in many town bathhouses seems to have*
> *been as common as going out to a restaurant was to*
> *become four centuries later. German bath etchings*
> *from the fifteenth century often feature the town*
> *bathhouse, with a long row of bathing couples eating*
> *a meal naked in bathtubs, often several to a tub, while*
> *other couples are seen smiling in beds in the mid-*
> *distance.*

Sounds like fun. But I have to confess that I rarely take baths these days. I enjoy the morning shower. I realise I'm setting a bad example to idlers. I'm sorry.

22

What Is an Idler?

WHAT, EXACTLY, is an idler? It's an excellent question and one that's been at the top of my mind for over thirty years (we produced issue one of the magazine in 1993). One authority on this tricky issue would be Dr Johnson. He wrote a series of columns under the byline "The Idler" in 1758 and 1759 which appeared in a weekly eight-page publication called *The Universal Chronicle*, a kind of cross between the *Week* and the *Spectator*. Other columns and mags of the day included the *Tatler*, the *Observer*, the *Rambler* and the *Wanderer*. The new breed of Grub Street hacks were getting paid to bumble around town and record their observations.

Johnson's Idler essays were themselves a way of avoiding work. He said he took on the job as a result of an "aversion to a labour he had undertaken" which was an edition of Shakespeare. (This is quite a good trick: in order to get something done, start one project as a way of avoiding another project.)

In the first essay, which was published on Saturday 15 April, 1758, Johnson outlined the characteristics of an idler.

The Idler, he says, is an Epicurean insofar as he is happy with the bare necessities. The Idler is "satisfied with what he can most easily obtain". This is good because he or she "escapes labours which are often fruitless, but sometimes succeeds better than those who despise all that is within their reach". (A recent version of this idea can be found in the 1970s utterances of Johnny Rotten: "I don't want a big house in the country," I remember him saying in an interview, now archived on YouTube. "I'm very happy where I am.")

Idlers are not exactly lazy, Dr Johnson says, they are capable of intense bouts of concentrated labour. "The diligence of an Idler is rapid and impetuous." The way they work has something in common with the principle of momentum: there is a long period of reflection and thought and procrastination before the real work starts, just as "ponderous bodies forced into velocity move with a violence proportionate to their own weight."

We might make another definition, which is to choose something you enjoy doing and get someone to pay you to do it. "Find a job you love and you'll never work again," as they say.

"Work" could be defined as something you don't want to do. If you *do* want to do it – whatever it is, and it could be banking – then it's not work. As D H Lawrence put it in his 1929 poem "A Sane Revolution":

Let's abolish labour, let's have done with labouring!
Work can be fun, and men can enjoy it;
   then it's not labour.
Let's have it so! Let's make a revolution for fun!

Aristotle would have advised that it would be difficult to be a full-time idler because we all need money to survive. He said we need to work in order to create the leisure time during which to be idle. But that we should not overwork. He would have agreed with Bernie Sanders who recently said we should be aiming for a 32-hour working week.

In my case, I'm often accused of working too hard and being insufficiently idle for someone who promotes the idling creed. My answer to this is that I retired when I was 34. At that point I gave up all the work I was doing simply for the money and since then I have pretty much done exactly what I wanted every day. (And it's not always been easy, to be sure.) My work is play, and I will never retire, as I have nothing to retire from.

In the end perhaps being an idler is something to do with being mentally free, with having escaped Blake's "mind-forg'd manacles", and living a life with plenty of time for reflection and for aimless wandering. "The unexamined life is not worth living," as Socrates, the ultimate idler, put it.

23

Rage Against the Dishwasher

SOMETIMES I FEEL I'd like to chuck all the machines out of the house. Get rid of them. I'd use a large pestle and mortar instead of the Magimix, wash up by hand instead of using the dishwasher, and harness the sun and wind and the heat of the stove to dry the clothes.

I expressed similar feelings in a book I wrote many years ago, particularly relating to the dishwasher. And they didn't go down well. "What's this nonsense about not having a dishwasher?" I was asked by horrified readers at festivals. "You're supposed to be an idler!"

Back then I was living in a tumbledown Devon farm-house and we didn't have a dishwasher, even though we had three children and lots of people coming to stay. For me it was an ideological vision, possibly tyrannically pursued: go back to hand tools, medieval technology, wind power. No TV – card games and books instead. Chuck out the strimmer and buy a scythe. I did, in fact, do this. (Well, I didn't actually throw the strimmer away but I did buy a scythe.) At one stage I even contemplated getting rid of the car and replacing it with a horse and cart.

Back in London I gave up these ideals. I could no longer impose such crazy schemes on the rest of my family. I reminded myself of the awful controlling Dad in the Aldous Huxley story "The Claxtons", about a proto-hippy family living "the simple life" in horribly self-conscious fashion. So I happily went back to making full use of the dishwasher.

But last week the dishwasher went wrong. It would not drain. Now, Victoria and I consider ourselves dab hands at dishwasher maintenance. We've mended our own before, and we've mended the dishwashers of friends. So with great confidence we pulled it out, unscrewed the waste pipe, emptied the water, unscrewed a bit of plastic at the bottom and spun a little wheel around to dislodge bits of rice and broken glass.

Three times we did this, and three times we failed to fix the problem. Three times I raged and swore and got covered in stinking oomska from the pipe. So we gave in and called the engineer, who will charge God knows what to look at it.

While we wait for the engineer to come, we've been forced to do our own washing up and, weirdly, we seem to prefer it. No loading and unloading. No worrying that the dishwasher hasn't washed the glasses properly and has left a sheen of opaque residue on them, meaning they all have to be rinsed again. The dishwasher in any case only does the easy stuff, glasses and plates, which take about three seconds to wash up anyway. Pans need to be done by hand.

Our offspring are helping (they should be, they're all adults now). The washing up gets done quickly. It's not postponed. Hence the return of my latent anti-machine feelings. Do they really save labour? Are they not more trouble than they're worth?

Dishwashers have been hailed by their apologists as a liberation from washing up. But is this just a myth? Do they not in fact enslave us? Would we not be better going back to washing up by hand? And isn't this better for the planet anyway? After all, motors require fossil fuels to turn them.

24
Misery of the Seaside

THIS MORNING, I read – in a forthcoming piece [*Idler* No. 92] by our sheds correspondent Alex Johnson – the following lines from TS Eliot's "The Waste Land":

> *On Margate Sands.*
> *I can connect*
> *Nothing with nothing.*
> *The broken fingernails of dirty hands.*
> *My people humble people who expect*
> *Nothing.*

Those cheerful words, says Alex, were written in a seaside shelter in Margate in 1921 when the poet was 33. I wonder why the Kentish resort made Eliot feel so hopeless? Surely, at this point in time, less nihilistic souls were actually enjoying going to Margate Sands for a holiday? The twenties were a heyday for the seaside, and the classic tune "I Do Like to Be Beside the Seaside" had been written in 1907.

But it seems poets have never much liked being beside the seaside. I mentioned this poem to the Idler Academy's

Head of Philosophy Mark Vernon and he sent me back these equally gloomy lines from "Dover Beach" by Matthew Arnold, published in 1867:

But now I only hear
Its melancholy, long, withdrawing roar,
Retreating, to the breath
Of the night-wind, down the vast edges drear
And naked shingles of the world.

The poet goes on in equally miserable fashion. For him, the sound of the waves on the pebbles is deeply depressing:

Listen! you hear the grating roar
Of pebbles which the waves draw back, and fling,
At their return, up the high strand,
Begin, and cease, and then again begin,
With tremulous cadence slow, and bring
The eternal note of sadness in.

And Arnold reckons the ancient bards found the seaside pretty miserable, too.

Sophocles long ago
Heard it on the Ægean, and it brought
Into his mind the turbid ebb and flow
Of human misery …

What about you? Does the seaside make you feel gloomy or cheerful? I always thought I liked it, but now I've read these poems, I wonder whether I was deceiving myself, and that in fact there is something inherently and even eternally sad about coastal towns.

25
Joys of the Caravan

MANY YEARS AGO, we at the *Idler* produced *The Idler Book of Crap Holidays*. Editor Dan Kieran compiled fifty funny stories of hellish vacations, all sent in by readers. For the cover pic we chose what we considered to be a hilarious image of a middle-aged couple sitting outside a caravan with a power station tower in the background.

Well now it's nearly twenty years later, I'm approaching the age of the sad couple in the picture, and to me, their holiday doesn't look particularly crap. In fact it looks quite appealing. It's the caravan. I just love them, and so does Victoria.

Sometimes I think that all you need for happiness is a caravan. And maybe a folding chair. We're currently planning our summer hols and one idea is to rent a caravan in a field. We've done this before, in a lovely campsite on the Pembrokeshire coast in Wales. The caravan rental company delivers it, sets it up, and takes it away at the end of the two weeks. It has a little shower, a little kitchen, a little loo, a little lounge and a comfy bed. They're brilliantly designed and seem to have everything the caravanner might need. I wrote half of my book *An Idler's Manual* in one. An inexpensive, fun holiday.

We also have great memories of dragging a cheap old caravan round festivals each summer. It was a two berth that cost £200, less than a large tent, but which provided a lovely escape, a mini-home, in a busy festival. It was called an Abi Supreme, had been owned by the Red Cross, and we bought it from a breeder of fighting cocks just outside Stroud. It now sits gently rotting in a field in Somerset, home to a small group of sheep and hens.

I loved sitting outside our caravan on a folding chair, with a beer in my hand, staring at the sky or waiting for someone to stop for a chat.

And I shall arise now and go to Pembrokeshire
And a small caravan rent there, of plastic and
*   metal made.*
Two folding chairs will I have there, an awning for
*   rainy days,*
And drink real ale in the bee-loud field.

69

26

On Disappointment

I WAS CHATTING with a friend who runs a very successful small publishing company. He asked me if I had any books on the go. I replied, "I've got a few ideas out there, but doubtless they'll all come to nothing. Yet more disappointments."

"Yes. My life is one long catalogue of disappointments," he said.

And so it is. The project that we think might reach the fabled and mythical "tipping point" never quite happens. And this is true for the celebrated as well as for the obscure. Aldous Huxley was hoping until his death in 1963 for a major film or theatrical success which would give him financial independence. It never happened.

There are examples everywhere you look. I was struck that Bret Easton Ellis, speaking at an event in London earlier this year, said he spent thirteen years trying and failing to get scripts made into TV shows before giving up.

The brilliant Oliver Goldsmith was always hoping for a big success, but it eluded him. Worse, he never received the critical appreciation he hoped for, complaining that when he released a new book, "the public make a special point of ignoring it". Anyone who has attempted any sort of literary production will know what he means.

The other day I met a young TV producer. She said she was planning to quit the business. I asked why. "Too much heartbreak," she said. "Only one of maybe a hundred proposals sees the light of day. That's a lot of very disappointed people."

Rachel Weisz, in her interview in the current issue of the *Idler* [No.90], told me that for every success like *Dead Ringers*, she'll have ten disappointments. And Samuel Beckett famously looked back on his literary career with regret. "What blunders all the way. Why didn't I go into Guinness's as father wished?"

It's a thought that occasionally pops into the mind of anyone who has embarked on a more or less creative life, I should think. Why didn't I just get a job at John Lewis or in the civil service? The only response, I think, is a sort of cheerful Stoicism, and a counting of your blessings, and a giving of thanks for your freedom. As Epictetus put it, "Don't hope that events will turn out the way you want; welcome events in whichever way they happen: this is the path to peace." And disappointments, of course, can lead to good things, if treated with patience.

27

It's Official: Nappers are Cleverer

IT'S ALWAYS NICE when the science catches up with us idlers. A new report says that the more you nap, the cleverer you are. The findings were published in a journal with the appealing title of *Sleep Health* (I must get a subscription).

"We found an association between habitual daytime napping and larger total brain volume, which could suggest that napping regularly provides some protection against neurodegeneration through compensating for poor sleep," the researchers noted.

The report adds to a growing pile of evidence which suggests that, in the words of neuroscientist Prof Tara Spires-Jones, "sleep is important for brain health".

Sleep expert Matthew Walker carried out a nap experiment a few years ago. He gave a test to two groups of people. One group had powered on through the afternoon with no nap. The other group enjoyed a long post-prandial doze. The nappers did far better.

"Sleep not only rights the wrong of prolonged wakefulness but, at a neurocognitive level, it moves you beyond where you were before you took at nap," commented Walker.

So that's all clear. But the question remains. How to nap? Where should you take your siesta? And how long should it be?

Speaking personally, I find I can drop off almost anywhere. At school I would fall asleep at the desk during the first lesson after lunch. Sometimes the teacher would notice and bang the table to wake me up. At the *Idler* office I have a large chair in which I find I can enjoy very pleasurable short naps of about fifteen minutes. And when at home I either lie on my back on the sofa or on the bed and drift into paradise that way.

It's not always easy to nap in the office of course. That's why Michael Palin has said that every office should have a nap room. Progressive employers are now starting to introduce shorter working weeks. So maybe in the future Goldman Sachs will install chill-out rooms complete with orange beanbags and soothing ambient sounds, the better to improve the neurocognitive abilities of its staff.

28

Lament for the Old Trades

THE BIGGEST cheer of the recent [2023] Idler Festival came for poet Murray Lachlan Young after he performed what he called his semi-erotic folk poem, "The Fluffer's Demise". Sung in the style of Ewan MacColl, "The Fluffer's Demise" is told from the point of view of a fluffer. (For those who don't know, a fluffer is a member of staff on porn films whose job is to revive the male organ in preparation for a new scene.)

In Murray's telling, the fluffers all lost their jobs when Viagra came along. They complain that in the good old days they drank of the finest champagne, but now they're reduced to penury.

It's an old tale of course. When the printing press appeared, the trade of the medieval scribe, who produced those beautiful, witty, surreal manuscripts, came to an end.

Christian Brett, the *Idler*'s typesetter, is fond of the following quote which comes from a letter called "The Scribe's Lament" written in 1473 by a monk to the Doge of Venice. The writer, Fra Filippo de Strata, complains that the printers are undercutting him and are producing filth:

I, a scribe of good reputation, have been driven out of house and home by cunning printers. They print with no shame, and at a very low price, matter that inflames men's passions, while we scribes die of hunger. Cure this plague, if you will, by getting rid of printers. They persist in their wicked paths, setting Tibullus in type, while young girls read Ovid to learn about sin. These printers incite this behaviour because they make such huge profits from it. They flood the market with anything that hints of lasciviousness. Destroy the printing press I beg you, or these evil men will triumph.

In 1980s Fleet Street it was the turn of the printers to exchange champagne for water when the new technology arrived and was gleefully embraced by barons like Murdoch because it reduced his costs and enabled him to smash the unions.

Then the appearance of Facebook and Google saw scribes lamenting everywhere. I was one of the lamenters: my income from freelance journalism and books took a steep dive and then almost vanished completely. The newspapers cut their rates savagely. Why? Because the advertising money was all flowing to the two new monopolies.

The Internet is often compared to the printing press, but the comparison doesn't actually work. Thousands of printing presses sprang up around the world from the Renaissance onwards, and put the power of literary production into a wide range of hands. The Internet, by contrast, saw a wholesale theft of the world's advertising revenues by two gigantic corporations. In 2022, Meta sold £116.6 billion of ads, and Google sold £279.8 billion of ads. That's money that used to be spread out over thousands of media outlets across the world.

Speaking personally for a moment, I was always snooty about jobs in ad sales and preferred to become a journalist. However my school chum Nick Clegg had no such compunctions and he is now drinking of the finest champagne while I scrabble around in the Coop looking for bargains on beer.

Not complaining, I'm very happy. Just saying.

29
My Morning Routine

O<small>N A RATHER</small> nauseating podcast called *Coffee with the Greats*, which interviews absurdly rich American corporate executives, JP Morgan boss Jamie Dimon recently spoke about his morning routine. He says he gets up at 5am, reads about eight newspapers, and has one cup of coffee (no breakfast). Dimon then goes into the office and gets on with earning $34.5 million a year. (What on earth do they do with all that money?)

I wish these supposedly great people would just leave us alone with their guilt-inducing "early to bed, early to rise" parables. A couple of years ago a review copy of a book called *My Morning Routine* arrived in the office and made for very depressing reading indeed. Every single one of the successful people interviewed claimed they got out of bed at 6am or earlier. Typical examples: "I wake up at 5.30am. I drink a cup of water, eat my cereal, get dressed and run out of the door to work." "I get up between 4am and 6am, usually 5am."

The implied promise is that if you get up early, you will suddenly find yourself the boss of a gigantic corporation earning tens of millions of dollars every year. Well that's very obviously not true. The men at the top (they're generally men) are not there because they get up early, but because they are greedy, ruthless semi-psychopaths with no morals. And there are very, very few of them. They are famous because they are so unusual.

And anyway, early rising does not equate to real greatness. Dr Johnson was a far greater man than Jamie Dimon and he famously lay in bed till noon most days. Florence Nightingale was another renowned bedaholic.

My own morning routine would go something like this: Wake up around 8am and curse myself for the extra beer I had the night before (or for watching three episodes of an addictive American drama series). Lie in bed for a while and hope Victoria will bring me a cup of tea. Get my own cup of tea and go back to bed. Lie propped up by pillows, staring at the wall, trying to wake up. (At this point I am reminded of a joke my late friend the journalist Gavin Hills used to make. "I start the day with my morning workout. I try to work out who I am, where I am and what I did last night.") Get out of bed at around 8.45am and sit down for a poached egg and toast at 9am.

And we idlers are increasing in number, if a cheering report in today's *Guardian* is to be believed. A new survey says Britons are "less likely than people from elsewhere to place importance on work". The idea that hard work leads to wealth and happiness, long attacked by the *Idler*, seems to be losing its grip. Only 39% of UK respondents believed that "hard work would bring a better life" (that compares to 55% in the US, world leader in both the Protestant work ethic and of deaths through opioids). The piece added: "[Brits] also increasingly believe that it would be a good thing if less importance were placed on work, a figure that has risen from 26% to 43% [since 1990]."

Yes, it seems Brits are waking up to the realisation that the Greek idea of leisure, or *skole* – time devoted to philosophising – is just as, if not more, important than work.

To rephrase Priti Patel, we are the best idlers in the world.

30

To Go Forwards, You Sometimes Need to Go Backwards

THE RENAISSANCE is a strange term as it implies that prior to this "rebirth", the European population was living in a sort of dark age. That's obviously not true, as anyone who has visited the glories and wonders of Florence will surely recognise. The Middle Ages in fact saw an explosion of creative energies, in architecture clearly (the twenty-six surviving medieval cathedrals in England alone show this) but also in art and music. At the Idler Retreat in Umbria this week we heard from Sandy Burnett how a medieval monk invented tablature and notation for music, and that music then was gloriously polyphonic, with vast heavenly choirs all singing different notes and harmonies.

There was technology too: historian Seb Falk has written a brilliant book called *The Light Ages* which describes amazing medieval machines – astrolabes, clocks and so on.

Business, meanwhile, was arranged around the guild

system, where the craftsman and the owners were the same people. Usury, though practised, was frowned upon, and cities were self-governing communes, based on the Athenian model (but without the slaves).

The system was by no means ideal: in the medieval city states, large swathes of the population (the "*popolo minu-to*") worked for guilds rather than being members of the guilds, and to be sure, there was poverty, there were single-parent mothers and there was violence in the streets. Most men carried a sword by their side.

But the culture was rich and imaginative and sophisticat-ed. The Renaissance grew out of it. It was both the flower-ing of the Middle Ages, and the death of a great period in history.

This was certainly the view of William Morris and his circle, people like Rossetti and Burne-Jones, who called themselves the "Pre-Raphaelite Brotherhood", because they were medievalists; they loved the art that came before Raphael, who lived from 1483 to 1520.

Being a medievalist, and consciously idealising the Middle Ages, was, for Morris and his mates, a way of attack-ing the dull utilitarianism and greed of his own age. Morris, whose Dad had made a fortune in the City from his shares in Cornish tin mines, had certainly profited from this dull utilitarianism. Morris senior died aged fifty when William was still a boy. When he came of age he was left with a pri-vate income of £900 a year (which would be over £80,000 today). But instead of going into the City himself, which might have been expected, Morris – whose nickname was "Topsy" – embraced bohemia in the 1850s. His medievalism, says historian E P Thompson, was "a revolt against the world of the Railway Age, and the values of Gradgrind. It posed the existence, in the past, of a form of society whose values were richer than those of profit and capitalist utility."

Later, in the 1890s, when he'd become a confirmed socialist, Morris wrote: "Apart from the desire to produce beautiful things, the leading passion of my life has been and is hatred of modern civilisation."

But – paradoxically – this hatred of his own time and love of a bygone age made him into a true progressive. Morris moved Victorian civilisation forward artistically, politically and philosophically.

31

Dreaming of an Idler's Paradise

THOSE OF YOU who attend our Thursday night "Drink with the Idler" events will know that our theme tune is an old hobo song called "The Big Rock Candy Mountains" by Harry McClintock. It's kind of an idler's theme tune, and paints a picture of a hobo's paradise, where cigarettes grown on trees and hens lay soft-boiled eggs. It was apparently based on a much earlier poem called "The Land of Cockaygne", a medieval peasant's version of paradise (memorably depicted in Pieter Bruegel the Elder's 1567 painting of the same name). According to historian AL Morton, the Land of Cockaygne was a pre-communist revolutionary concept which featured bohemian ideals such as equality between the sexes and no private property. The anonymous fourteenth-century author of the poem described Cockaygne as a land of no work, free booze and plentiful food. Maybe George Michael had it in mind when he wrote "Club Tropicana". As the poem goes:

There are rivers broad and fine
  Of oil, milk, honey and of wine
Every man may drink his fill
  And needn't sweat to pay the bill.

Another key feature of "The Land of Cockaygne" is free love. Monks and nuns cavort with impunity. At one point, after prayers, the nuns throw their clothes off and jump into the lake:

When the young monks see that sport,
Straightway thither they resort,
And coming to the nuns anon,
Each monk taketh to him one,
And, swiftly bearing forth his prey,
Carries her to the Abbey grey,
And teaches her an orison,
Jigging up and jigging down.

In this land of plenty, ready-roasted larks fly into your mouth and little pigs run down the street crying, "Eat me! Eat me!" One couplet runs: "No place on earth compares to this / For sheer delightfulness and bliss."

Harry McClintock's "Big Rock Candy Mountains" has much in common with "The Land of Cockaygne", with the added spice of authority figures who are comically disabled. George Orwell referenced the song in *Animal Farm*, when Moses preaches to the animals of a land called Sugarcandy

Mountain, "where we poor animals shall rest forever from our labours".

I beseech you to look up the lyrics of "Big Rock Candy Mountains" for quiet study and for learning on the ukulele.

32

On the Old Comedy

IN THE MIDDLE of tragedy, we need comedy. The comedy of fifth century Athens came to be known as the Old Comedy. It was about topical satire (the later New Comedy avoided identifying real people).

Old Comedy's best known practitioner was Aristophanes, who, as some of you will know, has a walk-on part in Plato's *Symposium*. Here he spins an elaborate tale to explain why love exists. In past times, he says, the world was inhabited by a race of hermaphroditic roly-poly creatures with four arms, four legs and two heads. These creatures zoomed around the world at great speed. The gods in the heavens became worried by their power and decided to cut them down to size. Zeus, Aristophanes says, took the creatures and severed them in half with a wire, in the same way you would slice a hard-boiled egg in two. These incomplete half-humans – now with only two legs, two arms and one head each – then roamed the planet looking for their other half. Hence love.

Aristophanes' plays were equally silly and fantastical. They were knockabout, almost pantomimic, and satirised well-known Athenians of the day. In *The Clouds*, an old man with debts sends his son to a philosophical school called the Phrontisterion, or "Thinkery". This is a school run by Socrates, or a caricature of him. The idea is that the son will become so well trained in the art of ingenious argument that he will be able to argue his way out of the debts.

Socrates is presented as a cast-iron loon, a bearded cult leader, who towers above ordinary people in a basket which is suspended above the stage, the idea being, clearly, that his head is in the clouds. In the play (certainly not in real life) he also charges astronomical fees. The play was performed at the Dionysia festival in Athens in 423BC, and Socrates (a pal of Aristophanes) was in the audience.

The story goes that non-Athenians in the audience were asking each other, "Who is this Socrates?" Whereupon Socrates stood up, both to identify himself and to show that he was indifferent to the quite savage teasing of *The Clouds*.

A second play performed at the same festival also savaged Socrates. In the *Connus* by Ameipsias, we read the following dialogue, which teased the philosopher for his simple garb and habit of going shoeless:

A: *Socrates – shining in a small gathering, eclipsed in a large – have you come to join us as well? Tough, eh? Where did you get that coat? No shoes on your feet. You're bankrupting the cobblers with your insults!*

B: *Still he'd rather starve than flatter!*

Another comic poet, Eupolis, wrote:

> *Yes and I loathe that poverty-stricken windbag Socrates who contemplates everything in the world but does not know where his next meal is coming from.*

Socrates remained Stoical in the face of these insults (though the word Stoical had not yet been invented), reportedly saying: "We ought not to object...to be subjects for the Comic poets, for if they satirise our faults they will do us good, and if not they do not touch us."

In other words, he's saying that the piss-taking dramatists might have a point, and if they don't have a point, then who cares?

So the Old Comedy is a bit like *Spitting Image*, which also parodied the politicians and celebs of the day, and *Not the Nine O'Clock News* (both produced by the avuncular John Lloyd).

33

Make Moderation Sexy

As a teenager, I remember liking a famous phrase from Blake's *Proverbs of Hell*: "The road of excess leads to the palace of wisdom." I took it as a licence to drink or take drugs to excess. Wisdom would surely follow. However, as Mark Vernon points out, Blake also wrote: "More! More! is the cry of a mistaken soul, less than All cannot satisfy Man."

So Blake wasn't recommending hedonism. I think he was just suggesting that people have to find their own path through life, make their own mistakes, and that there is no point introducing puritanical prohibitions (like "the war on drugs" or Prohibition in America, 1920–33). Less is more.

However the proverb, if it is one, has contributed to a myth that most of us have at some time been seduced by, which is that extremes are sexy. They're rock'n'roll. Diogenes, De Quincey, Jimi Hendrix, Sid Vicious: there's something enthralling and theatrical about people who take it to the edge. "Live fast, die young".

This morning on Melvyn Bragg's *In Our Time* the discussion was on Aristotle, and it was striking what a boring philosopher he is, in a sense (Aristotle, not Melvyn). He's all about the average, the halfway house, balance and moderation. The famous example of what he called the "golden mean" is the virtue of courage, which is the middle way between foolhardiness and cowardice. All very true, but how do you make these ideas attractive to the young?

If I was a young creative in an ad agency, and was tasked with creating a series of billboards to promote the great philosopher, I would propose the slogan "Make moderation sexy". Why should pushing limits be seen as cool? Certainly as you grow older, moderation becomes more attractive. In the search for *eudaimonia* – the Greek word meaning "good spiritedness" or "happiness" or "fulfilment" – excitement is to be avoided. Boring but true. Goodbye to saying, "Where shall we go now?" Hello to saying, "I think I'll turn in."

Blake's proverb should be rewritten for an older crowd. I suggest: "The road of going to bed early leads to the modestly appointed cottage of wisdom."

34
We Don't Like Mondays

"I JUST DON'T want to do Mondays any more," said Victoria at the dinner table on Sunday evening. She says she still gets the "Sunday blues", decades after leaving school. That Sunday-evening feeling of gloom never leaves some people, however much they enjoy their work, and perhaps that's why The Boomtown Rats had such success with their song "I Don't Like Mondays", in which Bob Geldof declared he'd like to shoot the whole day down (though the song is about a school shooting incident in America).

My favourite bit of white van graffiti echoes this hostility to Mondays. It's a very simple idea and often to be seen inscribed on the back door of a dusty vehicle. The letters "MON" are accompanied with a sad face, and the letters "FRI" are accompanied by a smiley face.

Victoria's desire to take Monday off was shared by the Birmingham shoemakers of the eighteenth and nineteenth centuries. They instigated the custom of Saint Monday. Suffering from headaches after the weekend's drinking, they saw no reason to go into the workshop on Monday. There would be plenty of time later in the week to catch up with orders, they reasoned. So Monday was for fun. And there must have been something doubly delicious in taking a day off when everybody else was working.

Writing about Saint Monday in the *Idler* in 2002, leisure expert Dr Douglas Reid quoted a street ballad from the 1790s:

> *When in due course, SAINT MONDAY wakes the day,*
> *Off to a Gin-shop straight they haste away;*
> *Perhaps at work they transitory peep,*
> *But vice and lathe are soon consigned to sleep;*
> *The shop is left untenanted awhile,*
> *And a cessation is proclaim'd from toil.*

The custom of Monday skiving became so widespread that by 1855 the *Illustrated Times* could run a cartoon showing a large crowd of revellers enjoying a boozy picnic at Hampton Court on a Monday.

The employment agency Reed has played on this general hatred of Mondays with their "Love Mondays" campaign. If you don't like Mondays, they argue, then rather than "shoot the whole day down", or haste away to the gin-shop or Hampton Court, it would make sense to look for a new job, and that's where Reed can help. If you really enjoy your work, then you would actively look forward to bounding in there on Monday morning.

While many of us would like to honour Saint Monday, and lie in bed all Monday morning with a nineteenth-century French novel, or drink beer at the skittles alley, it looks as if Saint Friday is more likely to establish itself. As reported in the current *Idler* [No.93], Wall Street executives are struggling with a move among their staff towards what we might call Idling Fridays. "Friday is just a dead day," said Nick Bloom, an economics professor, and the *Financial Times* recently ran a piece declaring: "Thursdays really are the new Fridays."

35

Work: The Quiet Killer

THIS WEEK the International Labour Organisation (ILO), an offshoot of the UN, reported that nearly three million people die every year from work. Over three quarters of these fatalities, the ILO says, involve work-related conditions such as respiratory diseases, neoplasms and circulatory diseases. Another 330,000 people are killed each year in work accidents. Farming is the most dangerous sector: it kills 200,000 annually through fatal injuries.

The top "occupational risk factor" identified by the ILO was "exposure to long working hours" (defined as more than 55 hours per week) which was responsible for 744,924 deaths.

This story went widely unreported. Why? It's such a mind-blowingly huge number. Just pause to think through the enormity of the figure. To put it in perspective: jobs kill 47 times the number of people who lose their lives to war and terrorism each year, and ten times the number killed by drugs and alcohol combined.

And for all those millions who are killed by work, many more millions are non-fatally injured: the ILO reckons this figure is around 395 million. Those of you who have read about the Oxycontin scandal in the States will know that society's response to, say, an Appalachian miner's severe back pain, was to give him or her an addictive opioid and suggest they get back to work ASAP, thus making even more money for the feudal overlords through drug sales. The human solution would be to give the injured miner time off and improve the conditions so miners in future didn't get injured.

By any logical reasoning we should be declaring a worldwide war on work. Work should be made safer, hours should be reduced, and hit squads of UN officials should be swooping on unsafe workplaces and fining the greedy mill owners who profit from misery, pain and death.

The UK's working environments are relatively safe. Cambridge University's Professor Brendan Burchell, an expert on work and promoter of four-day-week trials, said that workplace deaths are 2% of what they were 100 years ago. But this is partly because the dangerous jobs have been exported overseas.

And Burchell stressed that work in the UK still causes premature death: "Nowadays a lot of people in the UK will be dying prematurely of stress-related illnesses in their 60s and 70s – people who could have lived good lives into their 80s. A lot of that pressure is caused by over-work and low-quality jobs where people are treated with disrespect by bosses, colleagues and customers."

Economist Guy Standing said: "We need to stop making a fetish of jobs."

Truly, idling saves lives.

36

William Blake: Artist, Poet, Anarchist

IS MAN A MACHINE or a spiritual animal? A mere collection of atoms or a godlike creature endowed with a non-material imagination and a soul? A complicated computer or a holy ghost dwelling in a physical body?

If you're William Blake, then the answer is clearly the latter. If you're some nutty avaricious Silicon Valley hyper-capitalist ad salesman-turned-prophet-of-the-future, then you probably believe the former.

Since day one the *Idler* has been infused with a Blakeian sensibility. The late great Gavin Hills used to quote the bard in his pieces for the magazine and today our resident philosopher Mark Vernon keeps the Blakeian flame burning.

As freedom-seekers, we hope to throw off the "mind-forged manacles" which Blake talks about in his 1794 poem "London":

I wander thro' each charter'd street
Near where the charter'd Thames does flow
And mark in every face I meet,
Marks of weakness, marks of woe.

In every cry of every Man
In every Infants cry of fear
In every voice; in every ban,
The mind-forg'd manacles I hear.

Of course this was written at a time when Britain was starting to congratulate itself on building what it called its "empire" by essentially raiding other countries of their wealth via the East India Company (you can hear William Dalyrmple talking on this at the Idler Festival). The Industrial Revolution was sending some children to "dark satanic mills" and others up chimneys. Greed and military might worked together to create profits and big houses for the few, all built on the tears and deaths of children:

How the Chimney-sweepers cry
Every blackning Church appalls,
And the hapless Soldiers sigh
Runs in blood down Palace walls.

We'd have to wait over fifty years before the arrival of the Factories Act of 1847, nicknamed The Ten Hours Act, which stipulated a maximum 58-hour working week for children. The mind boggles really; how many hours were the children working in mills before the act came in? The legislation was pushed forward by Lord Ashley, Earl of Shaftesbury (whose ancestor the third Earl of Shaftesbury was the famous philosopher) and by John Fielden, a cotton mill owner who said most mill workers died young:

> I well remember being set to work in my father's mill when I was a little more than ten years old; my associates, too, in the labour and in recreation are fresh in my memory. Only a few of them are now alive; some dying very young, others living to become men and women; but many of those who live have died off before they attained the age of fifty years, having the appearance of being much older, a premature appearance of age which I verily believe was caused by the nature of the employment in which they had been brought up.

Blake combined prophetic works with a sort of "antiwork" attack on the greed-infused utilitarian approach to the world, which not only produced unbelievable misery, but which also denied the life of the spirit. The Silicon Valley ad salesmen, money movers and data controllers – the Peter Thiels of this world – are the direct descendants of the textile factory owners of the nineteenth century. (To see an example of the utilitarian mindset in action, search "Willam Blake" on your computer. The first result reads: "Low prices on blake william blake – Amazon.co.uk Official Site".)

Thank God, in fact, for Victorian philanthropists, and for the likes of Marx and Engels and William Morris for shining a light on the appalling subjugation of our own people – as well as people overseas. And let's not get smug when it comes to our own age: the International Labour Organisation says that long working hours kill 750,000 people each year.

37

Caught by the Fuzz

THERE I WAS, happily pootling down Uxbridge Road on my bicycle one morning. Outside the tube station are two pedestrian crossings, strangely placed a few yards from each other. When one of them signals a green man, so – for some mysterious reason – does the other one. This is a real pest for us bicyclists, most of whom gingerly cycle on even if the light is red, when, that is, there are no pedestrians to be seen. The Deliveroo and Just Eat cyclists bomb through these lights at great speed, the quicker to deliver their over-priced cargo to the waiting customer.

The first of these crossings was showing a red light, but as there were no pedestrians to be seen, I blithely cycled through it. Ah, what a terrible mistake! There was a police officer lurking under the railway bridge. She beckoned me to stop.

"Do you know why I'm stopping you?" she asked.

I mustered all of my brain power.

"Because I went through a red light?"

"That's right. And I'm going to issue you a ticket. Please move your bike onto the pavement."

As she wrote down my details in her book, I became

aware of dozens of pairs of eyes focusing on this amusing spectacle.

"Have you caught many this morning?" I asked cheerfully.

"Oh yes, loads!" she replied.

I glanced at the ticket. I was shocked to read that the fine was fifty quid. I was even more shocked to see other cyclists bombing past us and through the pedestrian lights.

At this point I started to fume and rage.

"This isn't fair! There are two crossings here, right next to each other. When one goes, so does the other one. I cycle here every day and all the cyclists jump through the lights because half the time there's absolutely nobody here! Why don't you catch people up on the green where it really is dangerous?"

I ranted on and we were joined by a second police officer, to whom I repeated my rant. They argued that I was a danger to pedestrians.

I fought the law, albeit in a somewhat feeble manner, and the law won.

I eventually waved a cheery goodbye and went on my way.

I reflected on the ethics and morals of the situation. I felt a seething rage, like a child who'd been unfairly admonished at school. Should I stop at every pedestrian crossing, even when nobody is to be seen? I know that in sensible countries like Germany, red lights are obeyed even if the roads are clearly empty in all directions.

And actually I never jump red lights at junctions, only

these bloody pedestrian ones. That's the compromise with the law I had made with myself.

At the same time, I think my fellow cyclists and I feel it's absurd to sit stationary at empty crossings.

What would Socrates say?

38

Do You Really Need a Car?

You've got to love George Monbiot. In today's *Guardian*, he confesses that he goes around Oxford tapping on stationary delivery van drivers' windows and telling them to turn off their engines, so as to prevent global warming. It must be truly annoying for the drivers, to have this donnish corduroy-wearing puritan ticking them off: "Excuse me, would you mind turning off your engine? You do realise you're destroying the planet?"

George tells us about one such driver who did turn off his engine when requested, but did it "grumpily". I'm not bloody surprised! George was lucky not to get a smack in the face.

Still, while it's easy to laugh at Monbiot's priggishness, his anti-car diatribe has a real point – respect is due. He says that SUVs in particular are extremely dangerous, and kill more people than smaller cars. He says that cars are profoundly anti-social and I have to agree. Obviously for some jobs and some lives cars are essential. But do city dwellers really need them? Every day I cycle through west London and see fleets of gigantic Porsches and Range

Rovers clogging up the streets, and think how much better off we would be if they all vanished.

And it's not only the planet that cars are bad for. It's your wallet. Around 80% of car owners in the UK own their cars on HP. That means debt. My accountant says, "When I see someone driving around in a Range Rover, I just think, 'There's another person with £50,000 of debt.'" Anyone with a reasonable credit score can walk into a car dealer and walk out with a £20,000 brand new car having put down a two grand deposit and signed up for three years of monthly payments. That really is the height of stupidity. How absurd to borrow thousands of pounds for a hunk of metal that not only kills people but may be damaging the planet with pollution.

In 2014 the number of road deaths in the UK was 1,713 which – though a fantastic improvement from 2000 when the figure was 3,409 – is still a lot of people. The solution, as George says, is to drastically reduce the number of cars on the roads in our cities, and that could be done by introducing more electric trams and buses, and many more cycle lanes. I don't personally believe the answer lies in pedestrianisation: that can kill cities. Just look at the disaster of Leicester Square in London. Portobello Road hasn't been pedestrianised and is all the better for it. Besides, the stall holders need to be able to drive their vans along it to load and unload.

The problem, though, is that for many people, their car is intimately wound up with their status. Just as in days gone by, go-getters aspired to "a coach and six", so today the first thing people do when they get any money is upgrade their motor. A century of clever advertising has connected the car with notions of both freedom and worldly success – and I predict it would take decades to reverse that process. When you get in a car you feel in control. It's an illusion, of course, but you feel it nonetheless.

39
On Making Merry

D ON'T YOU LOVE the word "merry"? It's so medieval. It conjures up scenes of banquets with roasted swans, of jesters and tumblers, of fire-eaters in between courses and dancing to the melodious sound of the lute or pipe and drum.

The etymologists tell us that "merry" derives from an Old German word meaning "slow" or "leisurely", which is a lovely connection for us idlers. It then turned into the Old English "mirige" meaning "pleasant or enjoyable", and then to Middle (or Chaucerian) English "mirie" where it took on something like its present meaning of jolly and

cheerful. Its noun, "merriment", was our word for "fun" before "fun" came along.

In Shakespeare's day "merry" seemed to acquire the extra meaning of "a bit pissed" (I mean "pissed" in the English slang sense meaning "drunk", not the American sense meaning "angry"). The word occurs 175 times in Shakespeare. *Henry IV, Part II* has the record number of "merry"s for a single play: a full fourteen. There's a nice singalong in Act Five: "Ah, sirrah! We shall / Do nothing but eat and make good cheer, / And praise God for the merry year."

The medieval hymn "God Rest Ye Merry Gentlemen" is not about a group of jolly males. In fact it means: "My dear gentlemen, I do hope that God will help you to remain merry." The same use is found in the following few lines from a servant in *Romeo and Juliet*: "Now I'll tell you without asking; my master is the great rich Capulet; and if you

be not of the house of Montagues, I pray, come and crush a cup of wine. Rest you merry."

I think "rest you merry" could be a good new sign-off for emails, as a replacement for "stay well" or "stay safe".

The phrase "eat, drink and be merry for tomorrow we may die" does not appear in Shakespeare or the Bible or indeed anywhere. It's clearly a version of the ancient injunction *carpe diem*, and is a sort of mash-up of two biblical quotes. One is, "A man hath no better thing under the sun, than to eat, and to drink, and be merry", a line from *Ecclesiastes*. And the other is, "Let us eat and drink; for tomorrow we shall die" from *Isiah*.

These days "merry" is usually only used next to "Christmas" and "England". In the case of Christmas, I think it's significant that we use a medieval and Tudor word for what is a medieval and Tudor custom, revived and then morphed into its current form by people like Dickens in the nineteenth century. The British Royal Family use the less fun synonym "happy" next to Christmas, presumably because the word "merry" has connotations of medieval Popishness and superstition.

"Merry England" was so-called because in the years 1350 to 1520, the English calendar was stuffed full of days off. There were nonstop feast days and festivals and games. The maypole is the famous example of this outburst of joyfulness in the period preceding the more sober Reformation.

40

On Discovering Tennis in Middle Age

WHEN I WAS at university, my friend Justin took me to the gym. The year was 1988. Justin was studying Classics and, in homage to the Spartans, he had a green mohawk and the finely toned torso of an ancient Greek warrior. He was keen to rid me of my foppish ways and skinny physique. So I spent half an hour under his stern direction, huffing and puffing on various fearsome metal contraptions. In the changing room I started feeling sick and dizzy and had to sit down. The feeling lasted for a couple of hours. I never went to a gym again. I suppose I'm more Athenian than Spartan.

I didn't take any exercise, beyond dancing at raves and later going for walks, chopping logs, gardening and house-work, for the next twenty-five years or so. However, I've recently started to enjoy exercise very much. I don't go to the gym – perish the thought; all that narcissism – but I cycle to the *Idler* office and back most days. And to the off licence and back most evenings.

But the great new thing is that I've been playing tennis. And this is pure joy. I love it.

I don't understand the appeal of just running. It seems boring, lonely and a little pointless, and anyway, aren't we always hearing about runners suffering problems with their joints later in life? But tennis is fun, it's sociable, it's a game, you smile and laugh while playing. It combines exercise with making merry. I look forward to my weekly doubles game on a Sunday morning and the coffee that follows it.

While playing you forget about the rest of the world and your own insignificant problems. Tennis (alongside snooker) is also the best of all the sports to watch on telly. I'm starting to become slightly obsessed, and have even read two books on tennis, which present opposing philosophies. One is called *The Inner Game of Tennis* and takes a broadly Taoist "go with the flow" approach, and the other is called *Winning Ugly* and gives advice on exploiting your opponent's weaknesses. I hope to synthesise the two approaches.

I've also started watching long videos of Roger Federer knocking up, in the forlorn hope that some of his insouciant genius will rub off on me.

Anyway, I think the point is that as you get older, it's good to move about a bit. And there's another bonus: the more tennis I play, and the more I cycle, the less guilty I feel about the enormous amount of real ale I put away each week.